Mabel at the Table

Copyright © 2021 by Blank Cover Press

Text Copyright © 2021 by Lynda Modell ♦ Illustrations Copyright © 2021 by Jason Allen

All Rights Reserved ♦ ISBN 978-1-956249-00-2

First Edition, 2021

Published by Blank Cover Press

To all of the children I have had the privilege to teach over the years, thank you for helping me see the world through your eyes.
– LM

For Emily and Andrew
– JA

Mabel at the Table

Written by Lynda Modell

Illustrated by Jason Allen

Mabel got up from her bed.
"It's time for breakfast," her mom said.

"I'm starving," she squealed with delight,
"I'll eat everything in sight!"

Mabel, willing and so able,
Sat down at the kitchen table.

 Ate up all the apples there,

 Found some broccoli on a chair.

 Next a carrot, then another,

 Then a doughnut from her mother.

 As three eggs went down her throat,

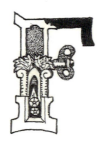 She nabbed a giant root beer float.

 The goose was a delicious sight,

 The ham got better with each bite.

"That's enough!" her mother cried,
But some ice cream Mabel spied.

 Jelly beans in every hue,

 She even ate a kangaroo.

 An enormous lollipop,
Lots of licks…she couldn't stop.

 A jar of marmalade she downed,

 Noisy nachos by the pound.

 A squiggly octopus came her way,

 Then pumpkin pie served on a tray.

 A careless quail was next in line,

 Fried rice made it taste just fine.

 A bowl of soup she wouldn't waste,

 Tomatoes added to the taste.

 She reached outside for some fresh air,
And grabbed a pair of underwear.

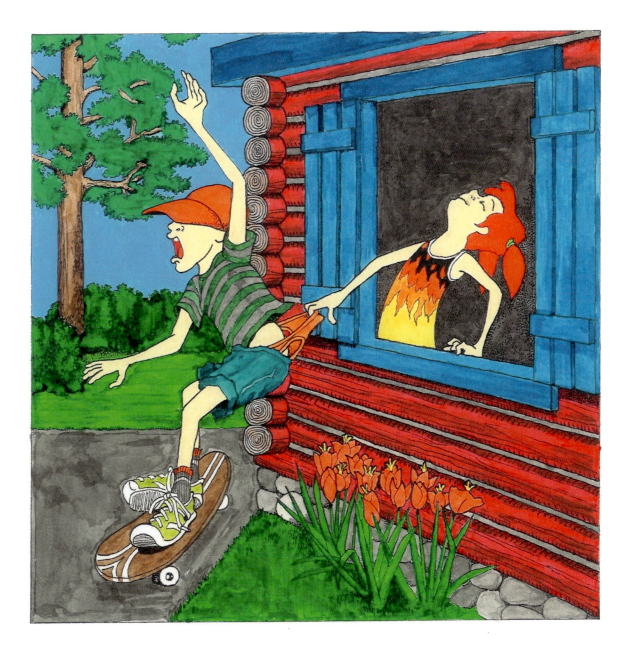

 She washed it down with vinegar,

 A bowl of
whipped cream made her purr.

Her worried mother called the doc,
And what he saw put him in shock.

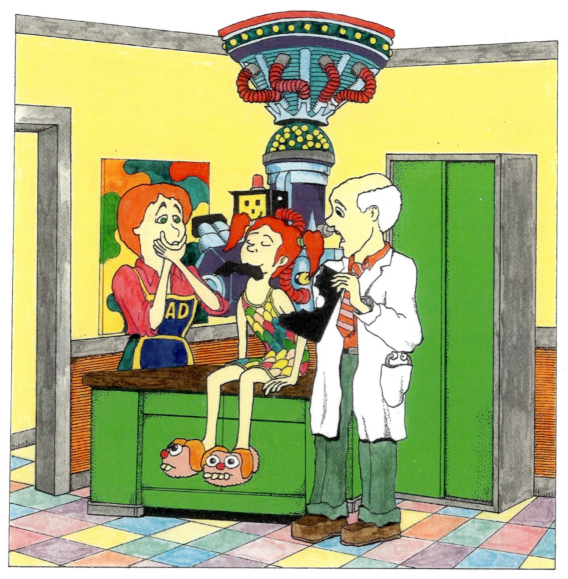

In his hand was her x-ray,
Down it went without delay.

 As some yogurt passed her chin,

 A zebra stew just went right in.

Mother begged her daughter, Mabel,
"Please, please, please just leave the table!"

"Mother, don't get all upset,
I just ate the alphabet."

Waddling to her room, she said,
"Call me for lunch. I'll be in bed."

About the Author

Lynda Modell is a former kindergarten teacher whose classroom was filled with laughter and joy. Her many years teaching children helped her create an unforgettable character named Mabel, who will bring smiles and laughter to the reader as she eats her way through the alphabet.

Growing up, writing was always an activity that Lynda enjoyed. When she began to work with small children, she realized how important it was to instill the love of reading in them, exposing them to as many books as possible and adding humorous touches along the way.

Lynda lives in Westlake Village, California, with her husband, where she spends her days reading, crafting, tap dancing, and working on the computer. *Mabel at the Table* is Lynda's first children's book.

About the Illustrator

Jason Allen is an art director/illustrator and lives in Simi, California. His two youngest children had Mrs. Modell as their teacher for five years...which is how Mrs. Modell and Jason became great friends.

Made in the USA
Columbia, SC
06 November 2021

48394816R00031